ISBN: 978-1-80099-334-1

Illustrations © Osian Roberts / osian99@gmail.com
Book design by Y Lolfa

Printed and published in Wales on paper from protected forests
by Y Lolfa, Talybont, Ceredigion SY24 5HE
tel. 01970 832 304
e-mail ylolfa@ylolfa.com
website www.ylolfa.com

Wales
IN
100
WORDS

y Lolfa

RHAGAIR / FOREWORD

Welsh is one of, if not the oldest living language in Europe and it is a miracle that not only has it survived, but that it is flourishing and evolving. It is also one of the treasures of Wales, defining and uniting us as a nation. This book is an offbeat collection of some special words and phrases unique to Wales. Some are ancient and derive from Early Welsh, and others draw on Wales's rich cultural and social heritage. However, as is the case with all living languages, there is a need to adapt to survive, and many terms in this book are new-born inventive creations guiding us through the digital age. Be aware however, as convenient as Google Translate may be, a language is more than words.

P.S. This book is just one of a large range of books about Wales, her language and culture, available from Y Lolfa. Browse our website, **www.ylolfa. com** and support your local bookshop!

Garmon Gruffudd

4

YNGANU / PRONUNCIATION

Every letter in Welsh is pronounced – there are no silent letters as in English. Most letters have only one basic sound, which makes pronunciation simple, but you will notice that all vowels can be long or short. The accent is usually on the last syllable but one. Here is the Welsh alphabet with equivalent English sounds:

A – as in h*a*rd or h*a*m
B – b
C – k
CH – as in B*ach*, the composer
D – d
DD – as in *th*em
E – as in s*a*ne or s*e*lf
F – v
FF – ff

G – as in *g*arden
NG – as in lo*ng*
H – as in *h*at
I – as in t*ea* or t*i*n
J – j
L – l
LL - as in *Ll*ane*ll*i. Place the tongue on the roof of the mouth as if to pronounce L, then blow voicelessly
M – m
N – n
O – as in *o*re
P – p
PH – ff
R – r
S – as in *s*ong, never as in a*s*
T – t
TH – as in clo*th*
U – roughly like Welsh *i*
W – as in b*oo*n or c*oo*k
Y – as in t*ea* or t*i*n or r*u*n

5

1 ANNWN

THE OTHERWORLD in Welsh mythology. Not the Christian influenced idea of 'hell' but a paradise of delights and eternal youth where disease is absent, and food is abundant.

2 ANSPARADIGAETHUS

NOT THE WELSH WORD for asparagus but a
flamboyant way of saying that something is
absolutely amazing.

3 AWEN

POETIC OR CREATIVE inspiration. In ancient
times the flowing of the awen was a state of
mind Welsh poets pursued and embraced.
Today it is widely used to convey the
inspirational muse of any creative artist.

4 BACH

NOTHING TO DO with music, it simply means
'small'. It is a versatile word that has many
uses, for example, as an affectionate way of
addressing someone – similar to 'dear' in
English.

5 BARA BRITH

A Welsh tea bread made with raisins, currants, and candied peel that literally means 'speckled bread'. It is traditionally flavoured with tea, and is served sliced and buttered at tea time.

6 BEIC BERFA

A COLLOQUIAL TERM for cargo bike. Literal
translation 'wheelbarrow bike'.

7 BENDIGEDIG

A WORD OF VERY HIGH PRAISE, literally
meaning 'blessed' but used as 'marvellous'
or 'fabulous' – whenever you want to give
something a five-star ***** rating.

8 BLODYN PI PI'N GWELY

A WELSH SLANG WORD for dandelion meaning the 'pee-in-bed flower'. Not as silly a name as it sounds as the dandelion was, and is still, used as a diuretic to help urine output.

9 BOCHDEW

Literally 'fat cheeks'. Probably the most accurate descriptive name for a hamster in any language!

10 BOLGI

Greedy guts. Someone who eats four Welsh cakes at a time. Literal translation 'tummy dog'.

11 BRAICH HIR

A WELSH WORD for a television 'remote control'. Literal translation 'the long arm'.

12 BUWCH GOCH GOTA

LADYBIRD. Literal translation 'little red cow'.

13 BWCI BO

GHOST OR BOGEYMAN. To Welsh children, however, the Bwci Bo can mean a goblin who haunts certain houses, mostly farms.

14 BWRW HEN WRAGEDD A FFYN

IT RAINS QUITE OFTEN in Wales and there are many words and terms to describe different types of rain. The literal translation is 'it's raining elderly ladies and sticks' but really means it's raining heavily.

15 CALENNIG

ANCIENT CUSTOM of giving gifts on New Year's Day. Children in many parts of Wales still carry out the tradition of calling door-to-door to sing a good luck song in return for a gift. Some dress up in a scary decorated horse's skull called 'Mari Lwyd'.

16 CANTRE'R GWAELOD

THE LOWLAND HUNDRED. An ancient lowland kingdom under the waters of Cardigan Bay that has been referred to as 'the Welsh Atlantis'. According to legend Seithennyn, the guardian of the sea walls, got drunk at a party and forgot to close the gate and the stormy tide broke through and flooded the whole area.

17 CARIAD

'LOVE OR DARLING', but much more meaningful than an expression in English such as 'Alright, love?' Also sweetheart, boyfriend or girlfriend. Used in Welsh and Wenglish alike.

18 CATH I GYTHRAUL

'A CAT TO THE DEVIL.' Similar to a *cat out of hell* in English. When you can't run or drive any faster.

19 CAWL

LITERALLY MEANS A BROTH or a soup. Can also mean a mess, a mix-up or a botched job.

20 CEILIOG

COCKEREL. Legend has it that on a visit to America triple harpist Nansi Richards met William Kellogg who was looking for marketing ideas for the cereal and Nansi told him that the name Kellogg sounded like the Welsh word ceiliog. The rest is history.

21 CERDD DANT

UNIQUE AND STILL VERY POPULAR Welsh tradition of singing lyrics in counter-harmony over a harp accompaniment. *Dant*, mutated from *tant*, a harp string.

22 CHWYLDRO

THE COMING WELSH SOCIALIST REVOLUTION. Do not laugh: it might happen sooner than you think. In the words of poet Harri Webb: 'Wales is marching backwards into independence...'

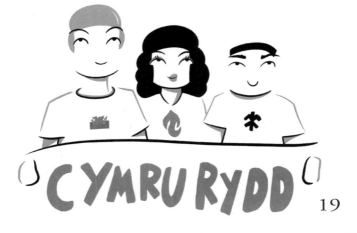

23 CHWYRLIGWGAN

CAROUSEL or a spinning top-toy. A classic Welsh tounge-twister to get your mouth muscles moving.

24 CO BACH

A TERM THAT WORKS WELL as it has two completely different meanings: USB stick or a likeable character from Caernarfon. Translation: 'little memory' or 'little Cofi'.

25 CLATSHO BANT

CLATSHO is one of many words in Welsh for fighting. 'Clatsho bant' means to start off, similar to the term 'fire away' in English.

26 CNAPAN

A VIOLENT, CHAOTIC AND LAWLESS ball game
played in western Wales between neighbouring
villages. Hundreds participated across miles
of open fields until sunset, often leading to
bloodied bodies, broken limbs and even death.
The precursor to rugby.

27 CODI SGWARNOGOD

RAISING HARES, meaning going off the point or
to raise a 'red herring'. Hares are creatures that
hold a special admiration and mystery in Welsh
mythology – near Oswestry one can visit the
Shrine Church of St Melangell, patron saint of
hares.

28 CRACHACH

A DERISIVE TERM for elements of the Welsh Establishment – the posh and pompous elite who run media, arts, politics and academia in Wales.

29 CROMLECH

DOTTED AROUND WALES, these are prehistoric groups of stones consisting of one large flat stone supported by several vertical ones. The first solid man-made constructions, pre-dating the Egyptian pyramids by almost 1500 years.

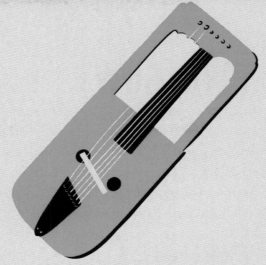

30 CRWTH

AN ANCIENT STRINGED musical instrument
associated mostly with Wales. With a broad
shallow body, it can be described as a 'rude'
violin. An acquired taste.

31 CWM PLU

LITERALLY TRANSLATES as 'feathers valley', it's one
of the many informal terms for bed in Welsh.

32 CWM SGWT

A HUMOROUS and slightly contemptuous name for a fictional place. Sgwt is a waterfall. Other examples are Cwm Rhyd y Rhosyn (Valley of the Ford of the Rose), Aberstalwm (Estuary of Long Ago) and the most famous of all, Dylan Thomas's Llarregub (read it backwards).

33 CWRWGL

CORACLE. A small, light, round boat made of wickerwork, covered with a coating of tar and propelled with a paddle. Designed to be used on the quickly-flowing streams of Wales. Still used on the rivers Teifi and Tywi.

34 CWTSH

THE MOST USED and loved of all Wenglish terms – loving hug or cuddle. Sometimes spelled 'cwtch', its many other meanings include 'to lie down' or 'a small cupboard' – hence, 'He was cwtshed in the cwtsh-dan-stâr with his wife having a cwtsh.' Cwtsh-dan-stâr being the cupboard under the stairs.

35 CYMRU

Cymru, the Welsh word for Wales, descends from the Brythonic word *combrogi,* meaning 'fellow-countrymen', whereas Wales derives from an old English word *wealh,* meaning 'foreigner' or 'stranger' that was given to Wales by the Anglo-Saxons.

26

36 CYNEFIN

'Habitat' is the nearest translation in English or 'heimat' in German. Somewhere a person or an animal ought to live, where the surroundings feel right and welcoming and familiar.

37 CYNGHANEDD

Strict measure poetry using a combination of rhyme and alliteration, literally, 'chiming' or 'harmony'. Though ancient in origin, cynghanedd has evolved over the years and has recently grown in popularity. The highest acclaim for a Welsh poet is to win the bardic chair for an 'awdl' (a very long poem in cynghanedd) at the National Eisteddfod.

38 CYTHRAUL CANU

THE DEMON IN MUSIC that raises its ugly head from time to time, especially during the fiercely competitive Eisteddfodau, causing jealousy, conflict and even violence among singers and musicians.

39 DAPS

In south Wales people don't wear trainers or slippers or football or rugby boots, they wear 'daps' (often with white socks – a Welsh Valleys fashion statement). Lee Trundle, Swansea City's striker, was famously nicknamed 'magic daps' for his fast feet and magical skills.

40 DIC SION DAFYDD

A WELSH PERSON who has turned his back on his roots, class, language and culture and imitates his masters. Similar to 'Uncle Tom' in America.

41 DIM GOBAITH CANERI

NOT A CANARY'S CHANCE, meaning 'fat chance'. An idiom that goes back to the coal mining era

when canarries were caried underground to test for poisonous gasses. The death of the unfortunate canary would be a sign that the miners should leave immediately.

42 DROS BEN LLESTRI

ITS LITERAL TRANSLATION is 'over the dishes', but it simply means over the top and can be used in any context.

43 DWYLO BLEWOG

Thief or 'light fingered'. Literal translation 'hairy hands'.

44 ECHNOS

A handy word meaning not last night but the night before. Other words in the same vein are echddoe 'the day before yesterday', trannoeth 'the day after tomorrow', trennydd 'the day after, the day after tomorrow' and tradwy 'in three days'. Etcetera...

45 EISTEDDFOD

OLYMPICS OF WELSH SINGING, reciting and poetry held in all corners of Wales. The National Eisteddfod is an annual event involving pseudo-ancient ceremonies and thousands of people wandering around a field. Strictly Welsh language but still enjoyable.

46 ENGLYN

TRADITIONAL FOUR-LINE VERSE in strict metre often compared to the Japanese haiku, but much more difficult as you have to rhyme and alliterate in 30 syllables.

47 ESGYRN EIRA

'SNOW BONES'. The patches and lines of icy snow that refuse to thaw as the weather improves after a period of snow.

48 GLO MÂN

AN IDIOM that derives from Wales's coal mining heritage. The direct translation is 'fine coal' but it is used in a similar way as 'nitty-gritty' in English.

49 GOG

NORTH WALIAN. From 'gogledd', meaning north.

50 GORSEDD

A COMMUNITY OF MODERN-DAY BARDS dreamt up by maverick Iolo Morgannwg but based on ancient druidic orders. The Gorsedd exists to promote the creation of literature, art, music and especially poetry. Can be seen parading in nightie-style costumes at the National Eisteddfod where they honour notable people.

34

51 GWDIHŴ

Owl. This evocative word is pronounced 'goo-dee-hooooo' and is one of the favourites when it comes to bird names in Welsh.

52 GWYNT TRAED Y MEIRW

'The wind of dead men's feet'. The term is used to describe a cold shivering easterly wind. Originates from the custom of burying the dead with their feet pointing eastwards.

53 HIRAETH

A FEELING OF LONGING associated with displacement. An intense yearning to be somewhere you are not or a nostalgic desire for the Wales and the lost places of the past.

54 HWNCOMWNCO

NOTHING TO DO WITH MONKEYS. Simply means 'him over there'. (See *Manamanamwnci*.)

55 HWNTW

A PERSON FROM THE SOUTH OF WALES. Derives from 'tu hwnt' meaning 'far over there' or 'beyond'.

56 HWYL

IN WELSH IT SIMPLY MEANS 'FUN', similar to the Irish *craic*, to express a sense of energy, enjoyment and fervour. Used by rugby pundits to convey a perceived unique Welsh form of team spirit and passion – but it's also a very popular way of saying 'Good-bye'.

57 IECHYD DA!

THE STANDARD WELSH DRINKING TOAST. Literally means 'Good health!' NB: Learn how to pronounce the *ch* properly (tongue at the back of the throat and breathe out with feeling). 'Iekyd da' just sounds like you're feeling icky.

A470

58 IGAM OGAM

Zig-zag. Most roads and paths in Wales are igam ogam and it's quite possible that after too many pints of Felinfoel or Wrexham Lager your walk home could be igam ogam too.

59 JAC CODI BAW

LITERAL TRANSLATION 'JACK LIFTS DIRT'.
Children in Wales soon cotton on to the idea
that JCB is an acronym of these Welsh words.

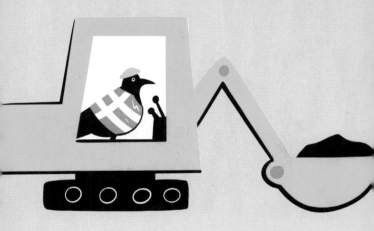

60 JIW JIW!

JIW JIW! OR *DUW DUW!* ('GOD! GOD!') is a
similar expression to *Gosh!* in English. Widely
used in both Wenglish and Welsh.

LLANFA
GWYNGY
YCHWYRN
LLANTYS
GO

61 A VILLAGE IN ANGLESEY with one of
the longest place names in the world.
Translation: 'St Mary's Church in the
hollow of the white hazel near the rapid

RPWLL LGOGER DROBWLL LIOGOGO CH

whirlpool of Llantysilio of the red cave'.
Pronouncing 'Llan-vire-pooll-gwin-gill-
go-ger-ur-chweern-drob-ooll-llan-tusilio-
gogo-goch' to tourists is a tired party trick.

62 LING DI LONG

To WALK, or to carry out a duty, lazily and without enthusiasm. The sound of the expression encapsulates the sense of aimlessness.

63 LLAETH MWNCI

MONKEY MILK. One of the many slang words for *cwrw* (beer).

64 LLWY GARU

A CARVED LOVESPOON that is presented as a romantic gift, especially at weddings. Traditionally it was intended to showcase the skill and patience of the carver, however it has morphed into a lucrative all-year gift enterprise.

65 LLWYTH DYN DIOG

A LAZY MAN'S LOAD. For example, when a work-shy waiter grapples with too many dishes to save a second journey.

66 LLYNCU MUL

To sulk or to be fed up. The literal
translation is 'to swallow a donkey'.

67 M.O.M. – MAS O 'MA

Means 'Out of here'. A rallying call to move
on to the next bar, or a plea for others to do so,
so you can have some peace at last.

68 MABINOGION

EPIC TALES full of romance, fantasy, humour and philosophy that have been passed down through the generations by word of mouth. Compiled in the thirteenth century these are the oldest surviving prose stories of the literature of Britain.

69 MANAMANA-MWNCI

'MIGHT AS WELL A MONKEY'. Used to suggest a slightly irresponsible, unproven solution to a problem, or way out of a situation. 'Hell, let's give it a go!'

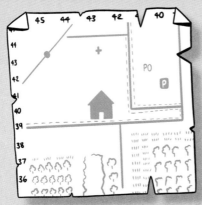

70 MILLTIR SGWÂR

IT IS SAID THAT EVERY WELSH PERSON has a
'milltir sgwâr' (square mile): the neighbourhood
or patch of land that you identify with and feel
at home in. Similar but not quite the same as
stomping ground in English.

71 NOSON LAWEN

A NIGHT OF INFORMAL, jovial entertainment full
of music, humour and story-telling held during
the long winter nights in rural Wales.

72 OMB!

A POPULAR ACRONYM on social media – 'O, Mam bach!' A Welsh way of saying OMG, meaning 'Oh, little Mum!'

73 PANEIDIO

PANED MEANS A 'CUPPA' of either tea or coffee. Paneidio is the relaxing act of sitting down with family or friends to gossip and to 'rhoi'r byd yn ei le' (put the world in its place).

74 PENDRAMWNWGL

ANCIENT WELSH WORD meaning 'head over heels, topsy-turvy, headlong, helter-skelter' – and also 'madly in love' as in Steve Eaves's popular song.

75 PENDWMPIAN

To DOZE OFF. A melodic word that conveys what it means perfectly.

76 PENGWIN

PENGUIN. One of the few words of Welsh origin
to make it to the *Oxford English Dictionary*. The
literal translation is 'white head'. Doesn't matter
that most penguins really have black heads.

77 PENMAENMAWR

A TOWN IN NORTH-WEST WALES that can be
literally translated as 'head of the great stone',
also a Welsh term for a bad hangover.

78 PIBGORN

A WOODEN HORNPIPE made from elder. Mentioned in Hywel Dda's laws, it's one of the oldest Welsh instruments known. Although once popular with shepherds and drovers and often played with the crwth, its popularity has waned. Like the bagpipes, often referred to as an instrument of torture.

79 PILI-PALA

BUTTERFLY. Pila-pala makes you think of light fluttering wings. You say it 'pill-ee pall-ah'.

80 PLYGAIN

A BEAUTIFUL AND ANCIENT form of harmonic, communal carol singing traditionally held in churches early on Christmas mornings and also in early January. Especially prevalent in mid Wales.

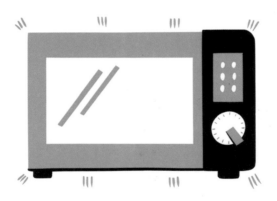

81 POPTY PING

A SLANG TERM for microwave. Literally means 'ping oven'.

82 PRYD O DAFOD

A BOLLOCKING. Literally means 'a meal of tongue'.

83 RANDIBŴ

'MYND AR Y RANDIBŴ' means 'to paint the town red', suggesting a gang of randy young men or women on a Saturday night warpath, possibly in Wind Street, Swansea.

84 SENEDD

THE WELSH WORD FOR PARLIAMENT. Slightly overwhelming for a talking shop in Cardiff Bay?

85
SHWMAI/
SHWMAE?

A GREETING meaning
'How are you?' Used
instead of 'Hi!' in many
parts of south Wales.

86 SINACH

A STRIP OF UNPLOUGHED LAND that is
frustratingly difficult to get to, or a chunk of
grass you just can't get your mower to cut.
These days the term is more commonly used to
describe a nasty or ill-humoured person.

87 SIONI BOB OCHR

ONE WHO SWAPS SIDES EASILY or pretends to support both sides. Often used in a political or sporting context.

88 TAFFIA

SELF-SERVING ELITE who pull the strings in Western Europe's last one-party state.

89 TRAED DAN BWRDD

'Feet under the table'. When someone has at last managed to get into the good books of the in-laws to be.

90 TWLL O LE

A dump or an unpleasant place, e.g. Milton Keynes. 'Twll' is the Welsh word for a hole.

91 TWMPATH DAWNS

A ceilidh without kilts.

92 TŶ BACH

Toilet. Literally 'small house'. Before indoor plumbing became widespread, most houses had a 'tŷ bach' at the bottom of the garden where one could contemplate.

93 Y LÔN GOCH

The 'RED LANE' down which food and drink travel from your mouth to your stomach.

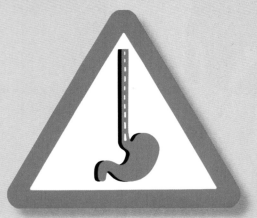

94 Y PETHE

A TERM for the civilised values, traditions and culture held dear and indulged in by 'enlightened' Welsh speakers. There is a Siop y Pethe in Aberystwyth selling all kinds of Welsh pethe.

95 (Y) WERIN

Folk, peasants. English terms for the working class can be derisive and divisive. In Wales belonging to 'y werin' is something to be proud of.

96 (Y) WLADFA

The Welsh colony founded in Patagonia in 1865, and still home to around 5,000 Welsh Argentinians speaking 'yr heniaith' with a Spanish accent.

97 Y MAB DAROGAN

AN ANCIENT WELSH BELIEF that a 'son of prophecy' will emerge to lead the Welsh to freedom. A number of figures have been hailed as Y Mab Darogan in history including King Arthur, Llywelyn the Last, Owain Lawgoch and, most famously, Owain Glyndŵr.

98 YCH A FI!

Yuck! Something really disgusting or revolting.
The 'ch' should be pronounced as the 'ch' in
'loch' and emphasised.

99 YMA O HYD

A FOLK SONG by Welsh legend Dafydd Iwan. The song's title '*Still Here*' is a defiant cry that Wales and its language, culture and identity have somehow survived despite all that has been thrown at it over the past 1,600 years and will be here until the end of time.

100 YNYS AFALLON

THE ISLE OF APPLE TREES: the perfect place to end. A mystical island in the western ocean of never-ending youth and sensual pleasure, where magical birds sing spell-binding songs and where King Arthur rests until his return. Cf. *Annwn*, our first entry.